Tomorrow is Another Day

Tomorrow is Another Day

By

Patricia H-F Moore

Acknowledgments

I would like to thank Turner and Anthony for their help in editing and formatting this book, and to the cover artist Sishir for his work.

OREIGN OFFIC

Contents

6 Tomorrow is Another Day

The Father Speaks English

The little girl stepped from the train onto the platform. Biting her lip, she rubbed her eyes looking around the empty train station in silent disbelief. She had never seen mountains before, or the snow that covered the fields beside the station- and hung on nearby pine trees, reminding her of an old-fashioned Christmas card. She drew a deep breath of crisp air smelling of pine mingled with horse manure. And what was that other smell? Soup!!! How long has it been since I've eaten, she wondered.

A stout rosy-cheeked woman sat waiting on a wooden bench. Pulling a wool shawl around her shoulders against the chill evening air, she got up and approached her.

"I'm Frau Eggler," she said, smiling. "Patricia?" The little girl nodded. Taking the small cardboard suitcase from her hand Frau Eggler led her to a waiting horse drawn sleigh. The driver took the suitcase, threw it onto the seat, and swung the little girl into the open sleigh, tucking a fur rug around her bare legs.

With a shake of the reigns the horses set off on a snow covered road at the edge of the dark forest towards lights shining faintly in the distance. As the sleigh glided over the snow Patricia rested her head on the side, burrowing deep under the fur rug, lulled to sleep by the clip clop of the horses.

She was abruptly awakened. "Whoa." The driver

pulled the horses up in front of a chalet nestled between tall pines and lifted her out of the sleigh. She walked hesitantly beside Frau Eggler down a snow-covered path to where a young woman stood waiting by the open door. The young woman smiled and nodded, "Bonjour," as she handed Patricia a pair of wool slippers to exchange for her snow covered brown leather lace-up oxfords which she lined up neatly beside the others in the hall.

Frau Eggler sat on a small stool by a coat stand in the hall and changed her outdoor shoes for slippers. Then she helped Patricia take off her new brown wool coat and examined the luggage tag attached to a button on the front. The luggage tag read:

Mr. and Mrs. Eggler

Grafstal, Near Kempthall

Winterthur

Switzerland

There was no return address.

Frau Eggler started to ask Patricia a question, but seeing the confused look on her face changed her mind.

In Patricia's pocket was a crumpled note written in French by her stepfather when she left London. It read:

This little girl speaks only English. Please help her to the trains to her destination. If you cannot help her please direct her to Cooks Travel.

W Frevelshausen. January 1947

***

Patricia had left the hustle and bustle of grimy Victoria Station in London on a bleak rainy morning three days before on the boat train to Dover. She was engulfed in a blur of smoke, loudspeaker announcements, and train whistles. Her mother bid her a hurried goodbye and pushed her up into a crowded compartment of the train. She asked a young man already seated and reading a newspaper, "Would you help my little girl find the ferry to Calais when you get to Dover?" The man nodded affirmatively, "Yes" and didn't speak again until they reached Dover some hours later. She sat opposite him between two sleeping soldiers watching as he read his newspaper, smoking one cigarette after another and grinding them out on the dirty floor.

She stared out of the train window at the bombed,

war torn landscape wondering where she was going now. She had only been home for a few months after she came out of the tuberculosis sanitorium where she had spent two years before mum sent her to her grandmother's in Yorkshire. She was settling into living in a house again at grandma's, and had started going to the local school. Then mum brought her back to London because the International Red Cross had arranged for her to convalesce in Switzerland. She'd never heard of Switzerland and wasn't quite sure what convalescing meant.

Once they reached Dover the man helped her find the ferry to cross the English Channel to Calais. She boarded the ferry clutching her ticket and suitcase, frightened by so many people pushing and shouting in languages she'd never heard before. The year after WWII ended people of all ages traveled though Europe looking for family members and loved ones. She wasn't the only child traveling alone.

The winter sea was rough and the ferry heaved back and forth making it hard for her to keep her footing. She made her way to the lounge below but was driven back on deck by the smell of stale cigarettes and vomit. A Red Cross nurse found her throwing up over the ships railing." Is anyone with you?" she asked. Patricia shook her head.

"Come with me. I'll take you somewhere to lie down."

The well-meaning nurse took her to the First Aid Station in the bowels of the ship that was filled with other sick travelers and lifted her into a hot airless bunk close to the ceiling where she immediately felt worse. "Have some barley sugar," the nurse coaxed. Patricia turned and threw up over the side of the bunk, this time all over the nurse.

In Calais, relieved to be off the boat, she continued her journey overland. She found her train and got a seat jammed between two old men in a crowded compartment, thankful not to be sitting on her suitcase in the corridor like less fortunate passengers. The train traveled day and night through France, Belgium, Luxemburg and finally into Switzerland. The trains screeched to a halt at each border where they were often delayed, sometimes shunted onto sidings, while border guards marched through the cars of the train shouting and roughly waking passengers demanding passports and visas.

Patricia watched the other passengers carefully to be ready when her turn came. Then she held out her passport and visa for inspection with shaking hands. She didn't want to be pulled off the train like some other protesting passengers she had seen.

She negotiated the ferry and trains for days across five countries from London to Kempthall, a Swiss mountain village without having to use the letter. She was eight years old.

***

Frau Eggler hung her coat on the coat rack opposite a staircase that disappeared into a dark hall at the top of the stairs.

"Kommen sie mit mir," she said, leading her down a long hall, past an open doorway. Patricia caught a glimpse of a shiny dark wood dining table with a big plant in the middle.

They entered a cozy kitchen warmed by a wood stove in the corner. She would have liked to warm herself but Frau Eggler led her to a chair at the breakfast table by the window. Looking out she saw a crescent moon and twinkling stars painted on a velvet sky. She didn't remember when or what she had last eaten as Frau Eggler set a steaming bowl of soup in front of her saying, "The father will be home soon. The father speaks English."

Tomorrow is Another Day

Frau Eggler led Patricia to a room at the top of the stairs and pushed open the door. Moonlight streamed through the window onto a bed set against the wall. The bed was covered with the biggest bedcover she'd ever seen, nothing like the thin tight counterpanes in the sanitorium. This was like an enormous white fluffy pillow covering the whole bed. She later learned it was an eiderdown comforter. Pulling off her clothes to her underwear she dropped them on the chair and climbed up into the bed. Sinking into the soft mattress and nestling her head on the pillow she pulled the comforter up to her chin.

There was a tap on the bedroom door and in came a friendly looking man with a bushy grey moustache wearing a dark striped suit with a shiny gold watch chain strung across his vest. His eyes twinkled like a genial Father Christmas as he approached the bed. He leaned over speaking in a strange language. She looked up puzzled, shaking her head. He tried a few more sentences, but seeing she didn't understand he gently brushed her hair from her face saying, "Tomorrow is another day," as though they would magically be able to understand each other then. That didn't happen. But slowly she learned Sweitzerdeutch to communicate with him and the rest of the family.

She woke late the next morning and tiptoed to the window looking out in amazement. Her room was at the front of the house facing snow-covered mountains and looked down over the pine trees where the horses had stopped last night. She dressed hastily and made her way downstairs to the kitchen. Frau Eggler greeted her and led her to the table where she'd eaten the soup the evening before.

A basket of black bread, a butter dish filled with butter, and a bowl of confiture - thick sweet red cherry jam - was waiting for her. Patricia had never tasted black bread or cherry jam and marveled at the dish full of butter. A tightly rolled napkin in a silver holder sat beside her plate. A small brown earthenware bowl with handles on both sides and decorated with red and blue mountain flowers was filled with creamy milk. She was relieved not to have runny boiled eggs with dry bread like she had in the sanitorium. The family started its day early so she ate breakfast alone watching the villagers pass by the kitchen window.

When Herr Eggler came home for lunch he said he would bring his friend who spoke English back after work that evening. His friend, Herr Fuhrer, spoke English as promised. They knew Patricia had been recently discharged from the tuberculosis sanitorium where she had spent the last two years because the International Red Cross had made the arrangements for her to convalesce with them.

She told them her mother lived at home with her older sister Pam, who was nine, and a baby sister Diane, and her father died a month before she left the sanitorium. With Herr Fuhrer's aid interpreting it was decided Patricia would call Herr Eggler Dad, as her father was dead, but call Frau Eggler Aunt because her mother was alive. A curious co-incidence was discovered. Aunt's maiden name was Anna Fischer and Patricia grandmother's maiden name was Annie Fisher.

Dad was to become Patricia's dearest friend. He was an accomplished skier and determined to teach Patricia to ski to help her recovery. He took her to the local ski equipment shop where she was told to stand and hold her arm at a forty-five degree angle above her head to measure the correct length for her skis. Then she was fitted with a pair of strong leather ankle boots and pair of ski poles, and was ready to begin.

Soon after they bought the ski equipment an old lady arrived with a long tape measure to measure the size of her chest, and the length of her arms. She talked with Aunt and then she left. A few weeks later she reappeared with a thick knitted jacket for Patricia to wear skiing. It was knitted in an all over square ribbed pattern, the body and arms dark green like the pine trees and the yoke brown with wooden toggle buttons down the front. Patricia was amazed to discover it had pockets knitted into each side. Patricia had never seen a knitted sweater with pockets before. "Try it on to be sure it fits you," Aunt encouraged her. Patricia was overwhelmed and could hardly breathe the words, "Thank you, Aunt."

Patricia slowly mastered the steep slopes at the edge of the village slipping, sliding and falling in the snow. Struggling up the mountain like a crab, one ski at a right angle then the next. When she tired of this she sidestepped up the mountain. Not as fast, but easier. At the top she pointed the long skis down the mountain and glided down to Dad's encouragement, and then as she gained too much speed he'd say, "Turn, turn, turn."

With the skis gliding under her and the sun and wind on her face she'd never been happier. War torn London was and her family faded into memory. She forgot to tell Dad and Aunt that she'd had TB in her ankle, and not in her lungs as they assumed, and had been bedridden with a cast on her leg and only recently learned to walk.

Sometimes Dad and Patricia took a toboggan with them when they went skiing. They pulled the toboggan to the forest at the edge of the mountain. Then they would speed down the mountain through the forest, weaving in and out between the pine trees, Dad in front, Patricia holding on tight behind him. The skis ran alongside the toboggan runners for extra speed as they careened through the forest. All was fine until one day a tree root stopped them in their tracks and they crashed into a pine tree breaking their skis and the toboggan. When they got home dragging their broken equipment behind them Aunt put a stop to their skiing, sledding expeditions.

Each day when they came home from skiing they entered the house by the back door and went down the steps into the cellar. A warm can of wax sat on top of the stove ready to wax their leather boots and the bottoms of the wooden skis then put in the rack ready for the next day. Ski jackets were hung on pegs to dry in the warm cellar. Sometimes the young woman Marguerite, the family maid who had greeted Patricia on her arrival, joined their skiing expeditions.

One morning in the courtyard in front of the house the little girl Patricia had seen watching her from the window in the house opposite said shyly, "I'm Sylvia. Would you like to go sledding after I get home from school?"

"I'll ask Aunt," Patricia said, and flew into the house to get permission. Aunt gave her permission and Patricia waited impatiently all day for Sylvia to get home from school. They pulled their sleds up the mountain and raced each other down.

Sylvia was a year older than Patricia and they became good friends. Sylvia's rosy cheeks and long yellow braids contrasted with Patricia's pallid face and straight brown hair.

She was plump and strong and Patricia was painfully thin, but that didn't stop them from competing on the steep slopes.

Sylvia's father worked in the office with Dad at the Maggi factory that made bouillon, what she thought smelled like soup when she first arrived. Later when she went on train trips with Dad and Aunt she always knew when they were approaching Kempthall by the soup smell trapped in the valley by the cold air in the surrounding Alps.

Aunt was delighted to learn that Patricia could knit and started her on a knitting project. Each day after lunch Patricia joined Marguerite by the stove to knit for one hour. Marguerite knitted innumerable baby clothes for her many sisters' babies in France, while Patricia knitted white or pink cotton socks. Patricia was very pleased with herself when she learned how to turn the heel without Marguerite's help.

On Mondays Aunt and Marguerite joined the other women at the laundry in the village center where they chatted and laughed together as they did the family wash. Big washtubs filled with steaming water were lined up in the washhouse under a sloping roof with open sides. Patricia and the other children who were not in school carried baskets of clothes to the clotheslines to be pinned up. Mondays were nice days.

Patricia liked the orderliness of her new life, where trains ran on time, and Swiss timepieces were known worldwide for their accuracy, unlike England where schedules were unknown, and trains came when they were ready.

Fire in the Valley

It was still dark when Aunt came into Patricia's bedroom and tapped her impatiently on the shoulder. "Wake up and get dressed quickly. We must leave right away.“ Patricia wasn’t told why but ate a hasty breakfast and left the house with Aunt and Dad while the sun was still struggling over the mountain. They walked quickly down the road without speaking in the chilly morning air to the train station.

The train soon came chugging into the deserted station stopping at the platform in front of them. They boarded the empty train and Patricia settled back to sleep resting between Aunt and Dad. It stopped at a village further along the valley and they got off.

The air was thick with smoke and the acrid smell of burning flesh. Patricia’s eyes burned as they walked to the village and she couldn’t stop coughing. “What is that smell?” she asked Dad.

“There has been a very bad fire in the cowsheds, and some of the cows have burned,” Dad said, taking a big handkerchief out of his pocket and tying it around her nose and mouth just like they did in London during the war when the houses burned after they were bombed.

When they arrived at the village Dad guided Patricia away from the cowsheds with the stench and sounds of moaning animals to a small tent where two women were assigned the care of the children. Patricia asked one of the women what had happened. “The cattle were brought into the cowsheds to keep out of the freezing cold but the cowsheds caught on fire and some of them were burned.” The other woman added,” Some of the houses caught on fire too and people were hurt.” Beside the children’s tent a Red Cross tent was set up to take care of the people who had been injured in the fire, and a third tent was being set up with food.

Patricia watched through an opening in the tent as people hurried back and forth all day between the tents and the houses. Occasionally she caught sight of Aunt or Dad as they helped injured people into the Red Cross tent. They worked with their neighbors from the surrounding villages all day helping those who had been burned while trying to put out the disastrous fire.

At noon the women ushered the children to the food tent where sausages were sizzling on a grill. They were served on long buns with mustard and sauerkraut. The sausages smelled like the burning air around them and Patricia felt sick. ”I’m not hungry,” she told her caretaker. “I’ll just have some milk." She slowly sipped the cup of milk wondering if it had come from one of the dead or dying cows in the cowshed. Years later she avoided the grills at barbeques and cookouts, preferring the salad bar instead.

At the end of the day Aunt and Dad came to collect Patricia. Their eyes were red and their clothes were covered in grease and soot. "Time to go home Patricia." Aunt said. "There is nothing more we can do here today." They fell asleep on the train back to Kempthall that evening while she sat wide-eyed looking at them. As they got off the train the comforting smell of soup greeted them.

No one spoke as they walked slowly back up the mountain with their clothes streaked with grease and the smell of burned flesh in their nostrils. Patricia wanted to cry but no tears came. She'd learned a long time ago when the bombs fell on London during the war, and people died in their burning houses, not to cry.

Springtime in the Mountains

The sun got warmer and the snow softened bringing ski season to an end, much to Patricia's surprise and disappointment. She hadn't expected the ski season ever to end. Spring arrived. The snow melted on the mountainside where she had skied and played on her sled, giving way to lush green pastures sprinkled with red and blue flowers. Cowbells were heard from sun-up to sunset.

Patricia came downstairs to the kitchen one morning to find a doll's pram with a doll tucked inside next to her chair. Aunt smiled.

"The doll and pram are for you to play with. Do you like them?" Patricia whispered, "Yes, thank you," hardly able to speak. She picked the doll out of the pram and sat it in her lap. She had a porcelain face with rosy cheeks, thick dark hair and blue eyes that opened and closed.

"I will call her Elsbeth because she looks like Sylvia's little sister Elsbeth,"

After breakfast she carefully undressed and re-dressed the doll. She shook out the covers and tucked her back in to take her for a walk in the fresh air. She pointed out the spring flowers to Elsbeth and told her to listen to the cowbells. After that she walked Elsbeth in her pram every morning.

In the evenings after dinner Dad worked in his garden

in the Paraguay, a vegetable garden with terraced beds cut into the steep mountainside. Patricia joined him walking through the valley across cow pastures, staying close as cowbells announced their owners wandering over to see them. In the Paraguay Dad planted vegetables and tended his beehives. He taught Patricia to pull the screens out of the hives without getting stung. She learned years later she was allergic to bee stings and on several occasions had to go to the hospital after being stung. They worked side-by-side digging the soil and planting seeds in the newly turned earth till twilight sent them back over the cow pastures home.

One day a woman arrived with a tape measure. She measured Patricia from head to toe - chest, hips, and waist - then disappeared. She returned with a partially completed dress in soft silky cotton with red Poppies and blue Gentians on a cream colored background. She pinned up the hem and measured the waist holding the pins in her mouth. She returned the day before Patricia's ninth birthday with the completed dress. The bodice draped over her chest and the gathered skirt fell softly on her hips. A Peter Pan collar framed her wind-burned face and short puffed sleeves revealed new muscles in her arms.

Aunt entered her bedroom the following morning, “Happy birthday Patricia. Today you must wear your new dress. Sylvia and her family are coming to celebrate your birthday with you.” Downstairs on the table was a cream covered gateaux on a glass cake stand like the ones she had seen in the village bakery. “Guten Geburtstag Patricia” was written in icing on top. It was the first birthday cake Patricia had ever seen.

The lady with pins in her mouth arrived again, this time with a partially completed red and navy small check wool skirt and jacket. She pinned the skirt hem and waist, then fitted the long sleeves into the jacket. The next time the lady with the pins in her mouth returned she brought the finished red and navy skirt and jacket with her. Patricia had never had a matching skirt and jacket before and ran upstairs to her bedroom to admire herself in the wardrobe mirror.

Spring brought with it a flurry of activity in the house. Aunt and Marguerite were busy taking up the smaller oriental rugs. They hung them over a line in the back garden where they beat them with a flower shaped bamboo rug beater, beaming with satisfaction as dust puffed out with each smack.

Aunt called Patricia, "I want you to go to the bakery for a loaf of bread. I don't have time to go this morning and we need it for lunch." Patricia's eyes widened. The family and her friend Sylvia understood her Sweitzerdeutch, but she hadn't tried it on a stranger yet.

Marguerite strapped a wicker basket to her back like the village children wore and she set off. The bakery was at the edge of the village where the path split in two directions. One path led to the bakery and the grocery store, and the other went down the mountain to the Maggi factory and the train station. She clutched the coins tightly in her hand and carefully rehearsed the words, "Ein brot bitte," over and over, all the way there. As she pushed open the bakery door the smell of warm bread greeted her.

"Guten tag." The woman behind the counter smiled at her. "Ein brot bitte," Patricia blurted out the words. The woman at the counter nodded as she took the coins and put the bread in the wicker basket. Patricia heaved a sigh of relief and started back home. After that was she was allowed to walk down to where the path split up to meet Dad at lunchtime.

Every day while waiting for Dad she watched the Italian factory girls running out of the Maggi works and clattering up the road in their brightly colored wooden clogs. She wished she could trade her brown leather oxfords for a pair of those brightly colored clogs.

Soon after her trip to the bakery Dad told her, "Patricia, Aunt and I think that you should go to school now and be with children your own age." Patricia didn't think this was a good idea at all. After she was discharged from the sanitorium and went home the neighborhood children avoided her like she was a leper. And when she went to school in Yorkshire the children made fun of her because she limped so badly after the cast was removed and called her "Stuck-up" with her London accent. She thought them ill mannered and coarse. And she couldn't understand the teacher who asked, "Have you left your wits in London, lassie?"

In the sanitorium a governess came to see her every day to help her with reading and needlework, while she watched with envy the children who could walk across the grass to the classroom on the grounds. Occasionally the nurses took their patients for walks in the spinney where the village children huddled around the gates watching them, whispering and nudging each other. Patricia was at an even greater disadvantage than the other patients because she couldn't walk with the cast on her leg and was wheeled on a stretcher. The patients performed for their audience by groaning and gasping till the nurses told them sharply to "Stop it. Or you will all be taken back."

She had only been at Keble Memorial *C of E* Primary School for Girls for the first year, and part of the second, when Tommy Murphy pushed her off the merry-go-round in the park. Her ankle got trapped underneath and was bruised and swollen when it stopped, and that had started the whole problem. Her mother rubbed olive oil on it, but it didn't stop hurting.

A few weeks later her ankle hurt so badly she couldn't walk, and it took her hours one day to get home from school. She scooted on her bottom resting on each doorway trying to ignore the air raid going on around her, and hid under a bush when one of the bombs sounded really close. She lost her gas mask which made her mother very angry.

When the pain got worse she stopped going to school and her mother took her to doctors, infirmaries and hospitals to find out what the problem was. After a year and a half Patricia was diagnosed with tuberculosis in the anklebone where it had been damaged from the merry-go-round, and was sent away to Harefied Tuberculosis Sanitorium.

Patricia remembered those unpleasant experiences and told Aunt," I don't want to go to school. The children will make fun of me because they won't be able to understand me." Aunt tried to reassure her but she was very apprehensive the following Monday when instead of knitting with Marguerite after lunch, she set off with Aunt for the village school. The headmistress and Aunt decided that she would attend school in the mid-morning to join the other children for gymnastics. Patricia was uneasy at first but the children were friendly and curious about her different language, and instead of making fun of her they wanted to be friends and hear her talk. She was relieved and looked forward to going to school for the gym class with the other children.

The Turnfest

Dad went off for two weeks every year to do his mandatory Swiss army training like all Swiss men. He kept fit in between by doing gymnastics at the Turner Hall with the other men in the village. In winter he skied on the local mountains and in the Austrian Alps with his friend Herr Fuhrer.

"You must get up early tomorrow, Patricia. We're going to the Turnfest," Dad said. Patricia looked puzzled. "What's a Turnfest?"

"Every spring the men from all the local villages compete in gymnastics. Dad wins many events," Aunt said proudly. The next day was Saturday and the sun was already warm as they walked down the mountain to the train station. They boarded the train with a large noisy group of neighbors to a far off village where the annual Turnfest was being held. The pastures outside the village had taken on the festive atmosphere of a fairground. Tents were set up with food and beer and an area with gym equipment was cleared for the contests.

Dad and the other men, young and old, took off their jackets and vests and rolled up their shirtsleeves. Names were called and they lined up to begin. They heaved the shot put and competed in jumping over the horse, balancing on bars, and doing fancy maneuvers on the box and other gymnastic equipment while Patricia and the women and children cheered them on from the sidelines. Patricia was practicing some of those same things at school and knew how hard they were even though the men made it look easy.

Patricia watched with pride as Dad was announced the winner of several contests beaming as his friends slapped him on the back.

When the competition in Dad's events was over they walked around the tents greeting their friends and neighbors. Then the smell of grilled sausages tempted them inside to buy the long buns filled with sausage and sauerkraut and covered with mustard. The grilled sausages smelled too much like the burning cattle last winter and Patricia nibbled on a bun with sauerkraut instead.

As the train pulled into Kempthall station that evening the soup smell that pervaded all winter, held by the cold air, had been replaced by warm summer air and the smell of cows now wandering in the pastures. Patricia walked close to Dad as they passed the beer garden at the edge of the village where laughing boisterous men relived their wins and losses at the Turnfest.

Mardi Gras in Zurich

Aunt woke Patricia early saying "Today is Mardi Gras. Put on your birthday dress we are going to Zurich to watch the parade with our friends the Urfers." After breakfast Dad, Aunt and Patricia walked down the mountain to the station to take the local train to Winterthur. The train had slatted wooden seats and the floor was clean unlike the English trains with their stained upholstered seats and floors covered with cigarette butts and ash. The train chugged through green valleys strewn with wildflowers and across roads where the stationmaster lowered a gate as the train passed by.

In Winterthur they changed trains for one with upholstered seats. As they left the small town of Winterthur the rural countryside and small villages gave way to the outskirts of Zurich. It was the first big town Patricia had been in since leaving her home in London. Unlike London, Zurich was clean and not bombed out.

In Zurich they went to the Urfer's apartment on Oberdorfstrasse where they were joined by Herr and Frau Urfer, and their eleven-year-old son, Willy. Willy was several years older than Patricia and she thought him quite handsome. He invited her into his room and showed her his drawings, which she thought were very good. "I am going to be an artist," he told her. "I may work for my father's advertising company." Patricia was very impressed since she had no artistic talents and had no idea what an advertising company was.

Willy's father called them and they left together with Aunt and Dad to make their way to Bahnhoffstrasse where the parade was to take place. Willy gave Patricia a chocolate bar but when she dropped the wrapper on the pavement the entire city turned and stared at her until she hastily picked it up and pocketed it.

The Mardi Gras parade marched in front of them; the sound of oom-pa-pa bands filled the air. It was the first peacetime parade Patricia had ever seen. The city was alive with genial adults and laughing rosy-cheeked children wearing colorful folk costumes. Patricia looked around in amazement at this fresh new world.

The girls wore red print cotton dresses with wild flowers embroidered at the hem and sleeves. White stiffly starched half aprons with a frill around the edge covered the dresses. The aprons were decorative like kind used on Sundays and holidays. On their feet were white cotton embroidered socks and wooden clogs, and a red skullcap embroidered with wild flowers completed the costume.

They were a vision in red and white sprinkled with

mountain flowers, each canton with a different costume. How Patricia envied those girls. The boys wore lederhosen and poet shirts with flowing embroidered sleeves. Red embroidered hats and long white cotton socks completed their costumes.

The trees created a dappled design on the sun-warmed pavement and the ornate bronze colored buildings glowed in the early afternoon sun. London flashed into her mind with its dreary streets, blackened, bombed-out buildings, and perennial grey skies. She shook her head to rid herself of those images, and watched Dad and Herr Urfer chatting and puffing on their cigars. The air was redolent with rich aromatic cigar smoke mixing in the light air with the smell of coffee and chocolate. The sun was hot on Patricia's head and the air chilly on her face. She buried her face in Aunt's soft fur collar wanting the day to never end.

As the parade wound down they started up the hill to the Urfer's apartment. Herr Urfer opened the front door to the dim vestibule where lengthening shadows fell on an antique Oriental rug that covered the mellow wood floor. He led the way into the parlor where the maid had laid out a cream-covered gateaux and coffee on a brass teacart. Willy and

Patricia tiptoed across the plush carpet past the grown-ups to the terrace and stood with their shoulders touching, watching the parade disburse.

A Handful of Nuts

"I want you to carry some apples down from the attic for Aunt." Dad motioned for Patricia to follow him upstairs.

She'd never been in the attic. Her bedroom was on the second floor next to Marguerite's bedroom. Aunt and Dad's bedroom was at the end of the hall. She had never been in either of them. Opposite her room was the WC with a door beside it she'd never seen open. It was the attic door. Her curiosity was aroused.

Dad opened the door and the musty smell of warm apples greeted them as they climbed the steep wooden stairs. Dust motes hung in the air caught by the sun as it slanted through the narrow windows. Patricia peered around the dim attic. On one side she saw a pile of suitcases with hers on the top. Dad led her to a large wicker basket in the corner that was half-filled with apples. So this was the source of Aunt's apples for the apple kuchen she baked for us.

"Hold out your apron," Dad said, and filled it with the apples. Then he walked to another wicker basket of hazelnuts, and scooped out a bowl to carry downstairs.

The hazelnuts were kept in a porcelain bowl in the leaded glass mahogany china cabinet in the dining room. The cabinet was locked, but the key was kept in the door. Occasionally Dad would lead Patricia into the dim dining room, open the cabinet, take the nutcrackers lying beside the porcelain bowl, and crack a few hazelnuts into her outstretched hands.

The little round nuts were a new taste. She'd only tasted English walnuts and Brazil nuts before, and then only the handful that came in her Christmas stocking. The hazelnuts were fragrant and delicate, not meaty like the English walnuts or heavy and oily like the Brazil nuts. Even the papery covering had an aroma and taste of its own. Patricia looked forward to these excursions into the dining room.

They never ate in the dining room but it was regularly cleaned by Marguerite. The room was dim with oversize mahogany furniture resting on a green oriental rug. After Marguerite had vacuumed the rug, Patricia's job was to separate the white cotton fringe at the ends of the rug neatly onto the waxed floor beneath. An aspidistra in a dark green pot sat on a table by the window between heavy damask draperies. It was dark and quiet like a church.

Patricia surveyed the dim scene that morning, her heart beating fast. Marguerite was upstairs making beds, and

Aunt was outside watering her cactus plants. She tiptoed into the dining room then quickly unlocked the china cabinet. She picked up the nutcrackers and cracked several hazelnuts into her shaking hands. Hearing the front door open she hastily replaced the nutcrackers on top of the nuts and closed the cabinet door. In her haste she carelessly spilled some nutshells on the floor.

So when Dad called Patricia into the dining room later and asked her if she had taken the nuts she burst into tears, ashamed to have taken something that didn't belong to her. Patricia loved Dad fiercely and couldn't bear to disappoint him. He looked down at her, his normally twinkling eyes serious, and asked her quietly, "Patricia, did you take the hazelnuts?" No words came out. She wondered if they would send her back to England to those grey, dreary bombed out streets.

Patricia loved Dad more than she'd ever loved anyone. But more importantly, she believed Dad loved her more than anyone else had ever loved her.

She had spent the happiest hours and days of her life with him. Had she spoiled it all for a handful of nuts? "Patricia," he said firmly, "The next time you want some hazelnuts you will ask me. Yes?"

Interlaken

"We're going to Interlaken for a holiday, to see our son Freddie, and our granddaughter Claudine," Aunt told Patricia smiling. Patricia bit her lip. She hadn't heard about Freddie or Claudine before, and she didn't want to go to Interlaken to meet them. Aunt brought Patricia's brown cardboard suitcase down from the attic. "We're leaving in three days so we have to get ready to pack. You will need your strong hiking boots because you will be mountain climbing," Aunt told her.

Dad said, "Aunt and I will stay a few days, but you will spend two weeks with Freddie and his wife Alice, and their baby Claudine." Patricia was silent. She didn't want to visit Freddie and his family, and most especially she didn't want to stay there after Dad and Aunt left.

Aunt packed all her new clothes, and a pair of sturdy boots she said she would need for mountain climbing. When the day arrived for them to leave Patricia put on her new navy and red skirt with the matching jacket, and went downstairs with her suitcase. She looked wistfully at the doll and pram in the hall and carefully arranged the covers over the doll as they went out the front door. She hoped the weeks would go by quickly, so she could come back to the house in Kempthall that she had begun to consider her home.

Dad carried her suitcase in one hand and his small

leather case in the other as they walked down to the train station. They took the local train to Winterthur where they changed to another train for Interlaken. Patricia stared out of the train window at the disappearing countryside that was taking her further and further away from Kempthall. At the end of the day they arrived in Interlaken, a resort city surrounded by mountains that people came to climb. The Jungfrau, a white snow-capped mountain, towered above the city and the other mountains. The peak was over fourteen thousand feet and always snow covered, and so high that often it was cloud covered. When the clouds lifted the townsfolk were always looking to see whether the Jungfrau was visible.

Freddie met them at the train station and hugged his parents enthusiastically. "Welcome Patricia," he said, bending over to hug her as she pulled quickly away out of reach, biting her lip so she wouldn't cry. Freddie was taller and slimmer than Dad with dark wavy hair and pink cheeks. His wore a navy three-piece suit like the grey suits Dad wore.

Freddie led them to a big black car and drove them through the busy city streets to his home, the Villa May. Patricia looked in awe at the imposing grey stone Italianate house surrounded by dense shrubbery and a black wrought iron fence. Wide stone steps led to a heavily carved wood front door that opened onto a spacious entry hall with rooms on every side.

Alice was waiting at the door to greet them, and threw her arms around Dad and Aunt, holding Claudine up for inspection. It was just as bad as Patricia had imagined. Claudine was a pretty blonde chubby two and a half year old who gurgled with pleasure at the fuss Dad and Aunt made of her. Alice kissed the air each side of Patricia's face saying "Allo, allo, Patricia, welcome to Interlaken. Please talk to Claudine in English. We want her to learn to speak English." Claudine already spoke German and French while Patricia could only just make herself understood in Sweitzerdeutch. Claudine was the same age as her baby sister.

Patricia was taken to a small cozy study filled with books from ceiling to floor that came off a large library. A narrow cot covered with cushions was pushed against the wall under a window, with bookshelves for the overflow of books on the surrounding three walls. When she was called for dinner she looked out the window onto the garden, pretending not to hear. Dad's voice came though the door. "Patricia, after dinner I want to show you the Kursaal. It's a very special garden." Reluctantly she got up and went to the door. Dad put his hand on her shoulder and guided her to the dining room where the others were already seated.

After dinner Patricia walked with Dad down the street to the Kursaal. She walked by Dad's side through the rose garden, and between the flowerbeds to the famous clock in the center of the Kursaal that was made out of flowers. A brass band was playing in the bandstand, and people sat on benches at the side of the rose garden, and on chairs set up on the grass to listen to the music. Dad found an empty bench for them to sit and enjoy the music together.

She never learned where all the doors in the villa led to, but spent much of her time on the wide semi-circular veranda that faced the back garden. It was like an elegant outside room with its black and white tiled floor, heavy wrought iron furniture, and colorful potted plants. Flowering pink and red shrubs, and neatly trimmed grass surrounded it, with a gravel driveway that crunched underfoot warning of anyone approaching. Breakfast and lunch was served on the veranda, but dinner was served in the dining room. The maid prepared the meals, but didn't join them as Marguerite did in Kempthall.

A few days later Dad told Patricia, "Aunt and I are returning to Kempthall. We will come back for you in two weeks." Patricia didn't want to stay there alone but didn't say so. She didn't want to hurt Dad's feelings.

Alice and Freddie treated her kindly and made her feel at home. Early each morning Patricia heard Freddie's footsteps crunching on the gravel below her window, and the motorcar start as he left for the bank where he worked, returning at the end of the day in time for dinner. Patricia joined Alice and Claudine for breakfast, then Alice tucked Claudine into her pram and they went shopping in the bustling city.

After lunch Claudine took a nap while Alice and Patricia relaxed on the veranda in the warm sun. Alice sewed or read and found some leftover red and blue knitting wool for Patricia to knit dolls clothes for her new doll. In the evening Alice stretched out on a big wrought iron chaise with overstuffed cushions to sing bedtime lullabies to Claudine.

Patricia curled up in a chair beside her, memorizing every word, which she sang to her doll Elsbeth when she returned to Kempthall.

Her other favorite room was the large paneled library that was filled with books. A deep red Oriental rug covered the floor, and there were big easy chairs to sink into." I think we have some English books somewhere on the shelves," Freddie told her. "See if you can find them." After much searching she found *A Tree Grows in Brooklyn*, by Maggie Smith, which frightened her although she didn't know why, and the *Salutation to the Dawn* by Kalidasa, which she learned by heart and later inspired her to later take up meditation, yoga and other disciplines to anchor one in the present.

Look To This Day

Look to this day:

For it is life, the very life of life,

In its brief course

Lie all the verities and realities of your existence.

The bliss of growth,

The glory of action,

The splendor of beauty.

For yesterday is but a dream

And tomorrow is yet a vision;

But today well-lived, makes

Every yesterday a dream of happiness

And every tomorrow a vision of hope.

Look well therefore to this day;

Such is the salutation to the dawn!

Kalidasa

Early Sunday morning Alice knocked on Patricia's door. "Wake up Patricia, we are going mountain climbing today. You must wear your strong shoes and take a sweater." Patricia dressed and went into the kitchen where Alice had packed a lunch of black bread, apples and dark chocolate for them, which she put into a rucksack for Freddie to carry on his back. Claudine had exchanged her white lambskin shoes for a sturdy pair of brown leather boots.

They drove out of the city towards the Jungfrau, which was visible today because the clouds had lifted. They parked the car and set off on a hiking path up the mountain. The path rose steeply and soon they looked down on the city below. The fields around them were carpeted with colorful spring flowers. Occasionally they passed other hikers and cowbells announced the cows as they hiked up the winding paths. Claudine walked sometimes, but when she tired Freddie carried her in a harness on his back trading the rucksack with Alice. When the sun was high they stopped at an outcropping of rocks for lunch.

Shortly after lunch they passed a small hamlet where the people looked at them suspiciously. Alice put her finger to her lips, "Keep walking Patricia, and do not talk to them. They don't like us disturbing them." A mile later as they passed an isolated hut Patricia looked in horror at a dead animal tied at the feet by a rope hanging upside down, its large brown eyes glazed over staring at her. She stumbled as she hurried quickly by to avoid looking at the blood-smeared animal she later learned was an antelope.

They climbed all day but the Jungfrau, now cloud covered, was no closer when they turned back to descend the mountain before the dark closed in. Claudine fell asleep in the car on the way home and went to bed without dinner.

A few days later Alice came into the library where Patricia was reading." I have a present for you," she said handing her a white cardboard box tied with a bright green ribbon. Patricia opened the box carefully pulling the tissue paper away. She gasped as she uncovered a dress. The dress was a fresh spring-green check-the color of Melmac dishes in the 1950's. The soft taffeta rustled as she touched it, making a delicious sound. It fitted perfectly and that evening she wore it as she strolled in the Kursaal.

She was wearing the green dress one afternoon as she walked along the main street in Interlaken. English boys in school uniforms whispered about her to each other as they walked behind her. Patricia waited till she was ready to cross at the light and then she turned and said haughtily, "I can understand everything you say, you twits," as she swished her skirts and slowly walked away.

Two weeks later Aunt and Dad came back to claim her as they had promised. Patricia was thrilled to see them and return to Kempthall. They boarded the train and had just stowed their luggage and settled down when the compartment door flew open and a group of noisy schoolboys crowded in on the seats around them.

As the train started off the boys burst out singing and yodeling. Patricia smiled shyly at one of the boys. He leaned forward and said conspiratorially,

"We've been mountain climbing all week. We climbed Kleine Scheidegg, and Grosse Scheidegg and lots of bigger mountains."

"I climbed Kleine Scheidegg last Sunday," Patricia told him proudly.

"Did you find any Edelweiss?" the boy asked her.

" No. We didn't climb that high," she replied. She knew edelweiss grew in cracks and crevices high on ledges at the edge of the mountains. They were the most treasured Alpine flowers because they were so hard to find.

"Then you must have one of mine," he said, untying a bunch of small furry white flowers from his rucksack, and pulling one out.

"Here you are." He leaned forward offering the edelweiss to her. She looked questioningly at Dad, who smiled saying,

" You must always accept the edelweiss when a young man offers it to you. He had to climb very high to find it."

Summer in Kempthall

It was summer when Patricia returned to Kempthall. She'd enjoyed her visit to Interlaken and climbing the flower-covered mountains on warm sunny days, but was happy to be back in Kempthall with Dad and Aunt again. But her stay at the Villa May had made an indelible impression on her, and became her standard for elegant living. Forty years later she built a veranda on her home much like the one at the Villa May where she had spent so many happy hours. She pressed the edelweiss into her bible where it remained a lovely memory.

One Saturday Dad pulled his bicycle out of the cellar where it had sat idle all winter, dusted it off and pumped up the tires. “We’re going to visit my friend Miss Liny,” he said. They set off down the path to the river Kempt at the bottom of the mountain. Patricia sat on the crossbar holding tightly to the inside of the handlebar with one hand while Dad skillfully maneuvered the bicycle on the path. Miss Liny was Dad’s secretary at the Maggi works and Dad had told her about Patricia.

Miss Liny greeted them warmly, and led them to a sunny patio overlooking the Kempt River, where she served them peppermint tea with gateaux. “What do you think of Switzerland? Do you like living here?”

“I like living with Dad and Aunt and I like their cozy warm house in Kempthall. I like the mountains and skiing and the fresh air, and I like Switzerland because it is bright and sunny, and there is not a war here."

When they left Miss Liny gave Patricia a Lindt chocolate bar in a shiny blue wrapper. Visitors often brought Patricia a chocolate bar when they visited their house, which she added to her collection of chocolate bars in brightly colored wrappers. She never ate them, but hoarded them in her drawer to share with her sisters when she went back to England. When they said goodbye Dad shook Miss Liny's hand, and Miss Liny kissed the air each side of Patricia's face. Then they walked the bicycle back up the mountain path home.

On warm summer evenings after dinner Patricia went with Dad to the Paraguay. The first mint was ready to be picked for peppermint tea, and the bees buzzed in their hives making honey. The carrots and beans they had planted in the spring were ready to be picked and would soon find their way into Aunt's soup or a delicious dinner. Patricia enjoyed mealtimes in the kitchen with Dad and Aunt, sharing the good food while Dad told about his day at the Maggi works.

Aunt cooked food that was new to Patricia like thick round pasta drenched in butter and sharp cheese, and a special favorite was mice: crisp fried cornmeal. Years later she learned that "mice" was maize, which sounded like "mice" in Sweitzerdeutch. Garlic was used to flavor many dishes and Dad ate a slice of black bread and butter spread with chopped garlic with his lunch every day. "To make his heart strong," Aunt said. Garlic wasn't used in Patricia's home in England, but it became a staple in her pantry years later.

One hot afternoon Sylvia knocked on the door. "The swimming pool will be opened this Saturday, and we're all going swimming," she told Patricia excitedly. "Come with us. We'll pick you up." Aunt overheard the conversation and said, "We must buy you a bathing suit." So the following morning Aunt and Patricia went to the grocery store where Aunt told the shopkeeper what she wanted. The shopkeeper pushed a ladder over to the shelves and climbed the steps to the top. She pulled a box from the top shelf and carefully placed it on the counter. Inside were several bathing suits in different sizes. Aunt looked through the box then held a dark green and brown wool bathing suit against Patricia's body. "This one looks like it will fit. What do you think?" Patricia wasn't sure about the color or the size, but since there didn't seem to be another option agreed. "I think this will be fine."

Saturday afternoon Sylvia came by as promised with some of the children Patricia recognized from school. They made their way to the swimming pool, which was next to the Turner Hall. Sylvia led Patricia to one side to the girl's cubicles and told her to change into her bathing suit. The bathing suit came high up on her chest and down to her mid thighs. When she jumped into the water the wool sagged and came almost to her knees.

Small white wriggly worms lined the edge of the pool, but since the other children ignored them she decided to ignore them also. The boys lined up at the side of the pool and raising their right arm in a salute shouted, "Hail Hitler. In case we lose," as they jumped into the pool one after the other. Patricia was startled. She had heard the grown-ups whispering about Hitler during the war in England where no one thought Hitler was a joking matter. Dad joined the men at the end of the pool where they did laps for a while, and then gathered in a group to chat.

Not long after the swimming expedition Patricia woke up one morning with swollen legs oozing with pus. Walking down the stairs was very painful. Aunt examined her legs but was did not know what the problem was. She tucked Patricia back in bed and that afternoon a nun arrived from a village a few miles away. She cleaned the oozing sores and applied a poultice and said to remain in bed. She would return the next day. The nun came every day for a week dressing the sores with the foul smelling poultice till they eventually stopped seeping and healed up.

Sundays Patricia dressed up in her birthday dress when they took the ferry on Lake Zurich or Lake Zug to Zollikon and Pfafflikon to join friends for garden parties and eat creamy gateaux.

The Green Dress

Patricia never meant to disappoint Dad but she did again. This time over the green dress Alice had given her on her visit to Interlaken. “Your green dress is getting too small for you. Would you like to give it to the little refugee girl in Lindau?” Aunt suggested.

"My dress still fits me. I don't want to give it away."

"The bodice is tight, and it is above your knees."

Patricia had an uncharacteristic temper tantrum at Aunts suggestion. But how could she tell her how much she loved green dress. She felt like a princess in the green dress after getting her clothes at the clothes exchange at St. Mathew's church during the war, and living in a nightgown for years. She knew she was being selfish but she didn't want to give it away.

The Christmas she was in the TB sanitorium when she was seven she had prayed every night for a red velvet dress, but Father Christmas gave her a book. Now Aunt was asking her to give up her green taffeta dress.

"Go to your room and wait until the father gets home," Aunt said. When Dad came home from work at lunchtime Patricia stood upstairs in the hall holding her breath and eavesdropping, and praying they wouldn't send her back to England, while Aunt told Dad about her temper tantrum. Dad called her downstairs to explain, but she couldn't bear the look of disappointment on Dad's face. So all she said was, "It's all right. The little girl can have my green dress."

Patricia Leaves Kempthall

The wise days of Patricia Fisher's stay with us will be over today. We shall miss her very much, as we liked her from the first day. She has never disappointed us. She always was cheerful, kind, obedient and every little work we gave to do, she did with cleverness. We often have had children with us, for instance from France, Austria, Alsace and our own country, but none of them we loved as much as the little English girl, our dear Patricia.

Not only we, her Swiss Daddy and Aunt, but also all our friends and neighbors regret that Patricia has to leave Switzerland. Our best wishes for a happy future accompany her on her trip home. We hope that once we shall meet again.

John and Anna Eggler

Kempthall

Switzerland

These words were written inside a small red photograph album with a white cross like the Swiss flag. Patricia sat alone on her bed in her house in London leafing through the pages of the photograph album wiping her eyes with the back of her hand. There were photographs of Dad and Aunt and their house in Kempthall, photographs of Dad skiing on the local mountains with her and in the Alps with his friend Herr Fuhrer. There were photographs of her skiing and sledding with Sylvia.

In the spring their were photographs of her in the cow pastures around the village, walking her doll in the pram, and riding with Dad on his bike visiting friends. Summer photographs showed her at the Mardi Gras Parade in Zurich and enjoying garden parties on Lake Zurich and Lake Zug. She was with Dad in many of the pictures since she seldom left his side when he was home.

Patricia carefully wiped the tears from her eyes. She didn't want to spoil any of the pictures Dad had so lovingly put together in the album that reminded her of that other, perfect life.

She had left Switzerland reluctantly, not wanting to pack her suitcase and leave this place and the people she had come to love so much, feeling guilty about not wanting to go back to England. Before she left the house she picked up her doll Elsbeth from the pram in the hall and carefully smoothed her dress, then she kissed her gently on the cheek as she put her back in the pram lovingly rearranging the covers. Dad and Aunt wiped their eyes as they walked down the mountain to the train station together for the last time for her to leave on her way back to England. Patricia bit her lip and held her breath to keep back the tears. Their neighbors were gathered at the train station with the children she had attended school with to wish her goodbye. She hugged Aunt and Dad and boarded the train when the stationmaster blew his whistle, straining at the window, waving long after they disappeared from view.

She found her way back on the trains and the ferry from Calais to Dover, then the boat train back into Victoria Station in a blur. Her mother was waiting on the platform when she arrived and she slowly got off the train. She wanted to tell her mother about the man in her carriage with crests of the Swiss cantons on his walking stick, but after not speaking English for so long she couldn't remember the words to explain it to her.

She shivered in her rain soaked brown wool coat as they waited for the bus to take them home. The bomb shelter still stood on the street outside their house, and gaps along the road where houses once stood were grim reminders of the war. The house felt small and cramped and the coal fire choked her. She resented sharing the bedroom with her older sister Pam after having her own room.

She missed the moon shining at night through the window while cuddled inside the big white eiderdown. She missed waking to the morning sunshine shining on the mountain outside her window. Her sisters thought her strange as she couldn't even talk to them now, and her baby sister Diane was no longer the little toddler she'd left behind but a little girl.

But Patricia had come back to England changed. No longer the sickly, clumsy girl who was laughed at and avoided by the other children, she was strong and healthy and loved and cared about.

Epilogue

Aunt and Dad visited Patricia after she returned to England, but with no telephone to let her family know exactly when they would arrive, their visit was untimely. They arrived at her house early one Saturday evening just as Patricia's mum was leaving to go dancing, wearing the pretty yellow blouse Aunt had had made for Patricia during her stay with them.

Aunt and Dad arranged for Patricia to visit them again the following year. She quickly and happily adapted to living in Kempthall with them again. Dad wrote to her mother asking if they could adopt her after discussing it with Patricia who was ecstatic about the proposed arrangement. Patricia's mother however, said" No", and insisted she return to London immediately. She went back feeling very guilty.

In 1951 Patricia came home from school one day to find an envelope on the doormat addressed to her from Switzerland. It was a black edged announcement of Dad's death. She went out and wandered forlornly through the streets mourning her loss she shared with no one.

In 1953 she sat in a London movie theater with tears streaming down her face watching Elsbeth, her old friend Sylvia's little sister, play the title role in *Heidi,* a Swiss classic. The movie director had wanted a village girl from the mountains to play his Heidi instead of a professional actress.

77 Tomorrow is Another Day

2783739R00039

Printed in Great Britain
by Amazon.co.uk, Ltd.,
Marston Gate.